Rising From the Ashes

Transforming Adversity into Leadership and Purpose

Dr Chibuzor Uwadi

The characters and events portrayed in this book are fictitious. Any similarity to real persons, living or dead, is coincidental and not intended by the author.

ISBN: 978-0-9563062-0-3

Wisdom Secrets Publishers

www.chibuzoruwadi.com
E-mail:hello@chibuzoruwadi.com

CONTENTS

FOREWORD

As a globally recognized executive leadership coach, I have had the opportunity to witness firsthand the transformative power of overcoming adversity and becoming a leader who makes a positive impact in the world. In Rising from the Ashes: Transforming Adversity into Leadership and Purpose, Dr. Chibuzor Uwadi masterfully captures the essence of this transformation, offering practical guidance and inspiration for anyone seeking to rise above their challenges and become a leader in their own right.

Through the principles of finding your purpose through faith and Ikigai, building resilience, using your voice and actions to make a difference, and setting and achieving clear goals, Dr. Chibuzor Uwadi provides the tools and guidance needed for readers to embark on their journey of growth and transformation. With real-life stories, practical tips, and transformational affirmations, Dr. Chibuzor Uwadi has created a powerful and inspiring guide for anyone looking to overcome adversity and become a leader who makes a difference in the world.

I had the pleasure of reading an advanced copy of Rising from the Ashes and was deeply impressed by the insights and guidance it offers. As a leader myself, I found myself resonating with many of the principles outlined in the book and was inspired by the stories of resilience and determination shared by Dr. Chibuzor Uwadi. This book has the power to inspire and motivate readers to take control of their lives and become the leaders they were meant to be.

I highly recommend Rising from the Ashes: Transforming Adversity into Leadership and Purpose to anyone seeking to overcome their challenges and become the best version of themselves. Whether you're dealing with personal struggles, professional setbacks, or a combination of both, this book will provide the motivation and guidance you need to rise from the ashes and become a leader who leaves a lasting impact and influence on the world.

FOREWORD

As rightly captured in the Scriptures in Job 14:1, "Man that is born of a woman is of few days and full of trouble." In addition to coming in various forms and ways, existential challenges have also brought some people to the point where they could not recover. In contrast, others could rise above their ground zero of existential realities and navigate through life successfully.

This unique book is one that one at ground zero of life's challenges needs to read.

In this book, Dr. Chibuzor Uwadi explores the journey of overcoming adversity and becoming a leader who positively impacts the world. The author draws from his own experiences and shares practical insights and strategies for overcoming life's challenges and turning them into opportunities for growth and leadership.

The book is written in a way that is relatable, insightful, and empowering. As the Secretary of Synod for six years for Dr. Chibuzor's father, Archbishop Rogers Uwadi, I can attest to the author's deep understanding of the human experience and the resilience required to navigate life's challenges. I strongly recommend this book to anyone facing adversity and looking for practical guidance on turning it into an opportunity for growth and leadership.

In the book Rising from the Ashes: Transforming Adversity into Leadership and Purpose, Dr. Chibuzor explores the journey of overcoming adversity and becoming a leader who positively impacts the world.

I encourage readers to take the lessons learned in this book and apply them to their own lives as they embark on their journey of rising from the ashes and becoming a leader who leaves a lasting impact and influence on the world.

Bishop Dr Chikwendu Ogan Igwe
Methodist Bishop of Abuja Diocese, Abuja Nigeria

PREFACE

Welcome to "Rising from the Ashes: Transforming Adversity into Leadership and Purpose." This book is about overcoming adversity and becoming a leader in your own life.

We all face challenges and difficulties, and how we respond to these adversities defines who we are. This book will explore the transformative power of trouble and its role in helping us grow and become stronger.

Through personal stories and practical tips, we will delve into the importance of resilience, emotional intelligence, and purpose in navigating difficult times. We will also examine the power of using our voices and actions to positively impact the world and the importance of leading with courage and vulnerability.

This book is not just about surviving adversity but about thriving and becoming a leader in the face of it. It will provide the tools and inspiration to help you embrace adversity as an opportunity for growth and to become a leader in your own life and the world around you.

As I sit down to write the preface for Rising from the Ashes: Transforming Adversity into Leadership and Purpose, I am filled with excitement and purpose. This book represents the culmination of a journey that has been both challenging and deeply rewarding. I am grateful for the opportunity to share my insights and guidance with readers seeking to overcome adversity and become the best versions of themselves.

Throughout my career as an optometrist, leadership coach, and global transformational speaker, I have worked with individuals and organizations from all walks of life. Through this work, I have witnessed first-hand the transformative power of overcoming adversity and becoming a leader who positively impacts the world.

In Rising from the Ashes, I share the principles and practices that have helped me and countless others to overcome adversity and achieve our goals. Through the principles of finding your purpose through faith and Ikigai, building resilience, using your voice and actions to make a difference, and setting and achieving clear goals, I offer a roadmap for personal growth and transformation.

This book will inspire and motivate you to take control of your life and create the fulfilling and meaningful existence you deserve. Whether you're dealing with personal challenges, professional setbacks, or a combination of both, you have the power to rise from the ashes and become the leader you were meant to be.

I am grateful for the opportunity to share my journey and insights with you. Rising from the Ashes will be a valuable and meaningful resource for you as you embark on your journey of growth and transformation.

Sincerely, Dr. Chibuzor Uwadi

PURPOSE OF THIS BOOK

The Purpose of this book, "Rising from the Ashes: Transforming Adversity into Leadership and Purpose," is to provide readers with strategies, tools, and inspiration for overcoming adversity and using it as a catalyst for personal and professional growth. Through thought-provoking lessons, real-life examples, and practical exercises, this book aims to help readers develop resilience, find their Purpose, and become influential leaders in their personal and professional lives. Whether you face challenges in your career, relationships, or personal life, this book is designed to empower you to overcome adversity and emerge stronger, more purposeful, and more successful.

INTRODUCTION

In life, adversity is inevitable. Whether it comes in the form of illness, trauma, discrimination, or other challenges, adversity has the power to shape our character and identity. But adversity can also be a source of strength and inspiration, helping us to find purpose and meaning in our lives. "Rising from the ashes: Transforming Adversity into Leadership and Purpose" is a book about how to turn adversity into a force for good, using it as a catalyst for personal growth and positive change.

Adversity is a natural part of life and can take many forms – financial struggles, health challenges, relationship problems, and more. While it can be tempting to try to avoid adversity at all costs, the truth is that adversity can shape and transform us in ways that can ultimately lead to growth and success.

In "Rising from the Ashes: Transforming Adversity into Leadership and Purpose," we explore how to turn adversity into a catalyst for personal and professional growth. We will delve into key strategies for overcoming adversity, building resilience, and finding your purpose in life.

As the author, I know firsthand the power of adversity to shape and transform. I grew up in a disadvantaged community and faced many challenges and setbacks throughout my life. However, through these experiences, I learned the value of resilience, determination, and the importance of finding my purpose.

Through this book, I share my journey and the stories of others who have overcome adversity to achieve their goals and fulfill their purpose. By reading this book, you will be inspired and equipped to rise from your ashes and create a life of meaning and impact.

Adversity is a part of life, but it doesn't have to define us. Instead, adversity can shape our character and help us grow more robust, resilient individuals. "Rising from the ashes": Transforming Adversity into Leadership and Purpose" is a book about how to turn adversity into a catalyst for personal growth and positive change. It's about rising and reclaiming your power, even in hardship or struggle.

We all face challenges and setbacks at some point in our lives, whether a severe illness, a complicated relationship or a personal crisis. But it's not what happens to us that defines us – it's how we respond to it.

Consider the story of Maria, a young woman diagnosed with a rare and aggressive form of cancer at 25. When she received the news, Maria was devastated. She felt like her life was over before it had even really begun. But instead of giving up, Maria decided to fight back. She underwent grueling chemotherapy treatments and surgeries, and through sheer determination and grit, she beat the odds and went into remission.

Maria's story is just one example of how adversity can be overcome through resilience and determination. And it's a story that is all too familiar to many of us. We all have our own struggles and challenges, but how we choose to respond to them matters. This book is for anyone who has ever felt knocked down by adversity but refuses to stay down. It's for those ready to rise, dust themselves off, and turn their challenges into opportunities for growth and impact.

"Rising from the ashes" is more than just a book about overcoming adversity. It's a guide to becoming a leader, using your experiences and voice to make a positive difference in the world. So, if you're ready to turn adversity into a source of strength and purpose, this book is for you. Let's start rising and making a difference together.

CHAPTER 1

Finding Your Purpose through Faith and Ikigai

One of the most powerful ways to turn adversity into something positive is by finding your purpose in life. Having a sense of purpose can give you direction and motivation and help you positively impact the world. But finding your goal can be challenging, especially in the face of adversity. It requires self-reflection and introspection, and it can be challenging to know where to start.

Faith and Ikigai are two concepts that can help you navigate this journey and find your purpose in life. Faith is a strong belief in something, often a higher power or spiritual force. It can provide comfort, direction, and drive in times of uncertainty and challenge. Faith is the evidence of unseen realities (Hebrews 11:1- paraphrased from the Bible TPT); it is a trust or confidence in something or someone that is often unexplainable or intangible Ikigai, on the other hand, is a Japanese concept that refers to your reason for being. It is the intersection of what you love, what you are good at, what the world needs, and what you can be paid for.

Finding your Ikigai can bring a sense of meaning and fulfilment to your life, and it is a powerful way to identify your passions and goals and align your life with your values and strengths.

It is essential to be open to exploring and trying new things, to listen to your inner wisdom, and to seek out advice from others if you want to find your purpose through faith and Ikigai. Finding your true calling may take some time and effort, so it's essential to be patient and enjoy the journey.

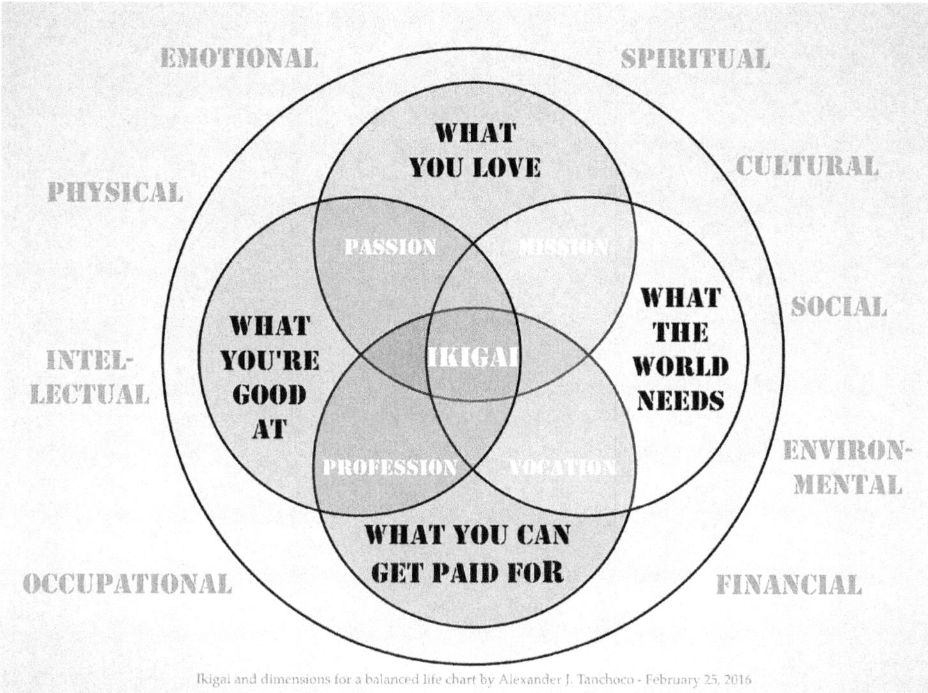

Fig. 1 (AlexaderJ. Tanchoco)

The journey of self-discovery and purpose-finding requires courage, resilience, and a willingness to embrace change. It is a journey that involves exploring your passions, values, and beliefs and using them to guide your decisions and actions.

STRATEGIES FOR DISCOVERING YOUR PURPOSE

Through Faith And Ikigai

1. Reflect on your passions, values, and beliefs: Take some time to think about what truly matters to you and drives you. What activities bring you joy and fulfillment? What values guide your decisions and actions? What beliefs do you hold dear and why? For example, if one of your values is compassion, consider looking for opportunities to work with organizations or causes that promote social justice or help those in need.

2. Identify your passions and interests. What are the things that you love to do in your free time? What topics or causes do you find most engaging and meaningful? Consider how these passions and interests align with your values and goals. For example, if you have a passion for cooking and believe in the importance of healthy eating, you might explore career paths in the food industry or start a blog or business focused on healthy cooking.

3. Consider your strengths and skills. What are you naturally good at? What skills and abilities do you have that you could use to make a positive difference in the world? For example, consider a career in environmental advocacy or public relations if you have strong communication skills and a passion for environmental conservation.

4. Think about what the world needs. What challenges or problems do you see in the world that you feel called to address? How might your passions, skills, and values intersect with these needs? For example, if you have a passion for education and a belief in the importance of equal opportunities

5. Explore opportunities for alignment. Once you have identified your passions, skills, values, and the world's needs, start looking for ways to align these areas. This might involve exploring different career paths, volunteering opportunities, or creating a side hustle or business.

For example, suppose you have a passion for writing and a desire to make a positive impact. Consider starting a blog or writing for a publication focusing on social justice issues. Consider volunteering with organizations that align with your values and goals. Remember to be open to trying new things and to seek guidance from mentors, friends, or professionals as you explore different options.

6. Explore your interests and hobbies: Explore new activities to see what sparks your curiosity and passion. Take risks and be open to new things, even if they seem scary or out of your comfort zone.

7. Seek guidance from others: Talk to friends, family, mentors, or spiritual leaders about your journey of self-discovery. Seek their advice and guidance and be open to hearing different perspectives and ideas.

8. Take small steps towards your goals: As you begin to identify your passions and interests, start taking small steps towards making them a reality. This could involve taking a class or workshop, volunteering, or simply setting a goal and working towards it.

9. Be patient and embrace the journey: Finding your purpose in life is a journey, and it may take time and effort. Be patient and embrace the process, knowing it is all part of your personal growth and development.

REAL-LIFE EXAMPLES

Finding Purpose through Faith and Ikigai

1. Mary had always been passionate about music but never pursued it as a career because she was afraid of failure. However, after much reflection and guidance from her pastor, she decided to take a chance and audition for a local music school. As a result, she was accepted and has since been able to turn her passion into a career as a successful musician.

2. John had always been interested in technology and enjoyed tinkering with gadgets in his spare time. So he decided to take a chance and enrol in a coding Bootcamp, where he discovered a natural talent for programming. He is now a successful software developer and credits his faith and Ikigai for leading him to this fulfilling career.

3. Sarah had always been passionate about environmental conservation but needed to figure out how to turn this passion into a career. After exploring different options and seeking guidance from mentors, she decided to return to school and earn an environmental science degree. She is now a successful conservationist and credits her faith and Ikigai for leading her to her purpose in life.

Consider the story of Vivian, a young woman who turned to her faith after experiencing a significant setback. Vivian had always been a successful student and athlete, but when she suffered a severe injury that ended her athletic career, she was devastated. She felt lost and purposeless and struggled to find meaning in her life. It was through her faith that Sarah was able to find hope and direction. She began volunteering at her church and helping others, discovering her passion for working with children. Sarah eventually went back to school to study education, and she now works as a teacher, using her gifts and talents to make a positive difference in the lives of her students.

Vivian's story illustrates how faith and Ikigai can be powerful tools for finding your purpose in life. Of course, it's not always easy, and it may require taking risks or stepping out of your comfort zone. But the rewards of living a meaningful and fulfilling life are immeasurable. In this chapter, we will explore the role of faith and Ikigai in finding your purpose and offer strategies for identifying your passions and goals. We will also discuss the importance of having a sense of purpose and how it can give you the motivation and direction to overcome adversity and achieve your goals.

Remember that finding your purpose is a journey; it may take time and exploration to figure out what is right for you. Be patient and open to trying new things, and don't be afraid to seek guidance from mentors, friends, or professionals.

TRANSFORMATIONAL LIFE LESSONS

1. Finding your purpose requires self-reflection and introspection. Take the time to consider what is most important and what you want to achieve. This might involve journaling, meditating, or talking to friends or mentors about your values and goals. Feel free to explore different options and take risks. For example, if you need more motivation in your current career, consider looking for new opportunities or starting a side hustle that aligns with your passions and values.

2. Faith and Ikigai can be helpful frameworks for finding your purpose. Consider your values and beliefs, as well as your passions, skills, and the world's needs, as you search for your ideal. Faith can provide a sense of meaning and direction in life, and Ikigai can help you align your passions and skills with what the world needs. For example, suppose you have a passion for writing and a belief in the importance of social justice. In that case, consider starting a blog or writing for a publication focusing on social justice issues.

3. It's always possible to find your purpose. Even if you have faced setbacks or are at a crossroads in your life, you can make a change and start living a more fulfilling and meaningful life. Refrain from letting your age, circumstances, or past mistakes hold you back. Instead, take inspiration from people like Jerry, who found his purpose later in life, and use your experiences and skills to make a positive difference.

4. Finding your purpose can give you direction and motivation and help you positively impact the world. Don't let adversity hold you back – use it as a catalyst for personal growth and positive change. Just like Maria, who turned her misfortune into a catalyst for resilience and determination, you can turn your challenges into opportunities for growth and impact.

5. It's essential to have a support system as you search for your purpose. Lean on friends, family, mentors, and other trusted

individuals as you explore different options and navigate challenges. A supportive network can provide emotional and practical support as you make changes and pursue your goals.

21 DAYS TRANSFORMATIONAL

Affirmations

Day 1: I am worthy of finding my purpose in life.

Day 2: I can make positive changes and pursue my goals.

Day 3: I will take time each day to reflect on my values and beliefs.

Day 4: I will explore new options and take risks as I search for my purpose.

Day 5: I will surround myself with supportive and encouraging people who help me to grow and achieve my goals.

Day 6: I will use my passions, skills, and values to make a positive difference in the world.

Day 7: I will not let setbacks or failures define me – I will use them as opportunities to learn and grow.

Day 8: I will cultivate a growth mindset and embrace challenges as opportunities for personal growth.

Day 9: I will practice self-care and prioritize my mental and emotional well-being as I pursue my purpose.

Day 10: I will be true to myself and align with my values and goals.

Day 11: I will not let fear or doubt hold me back – I will trust in my abilities and purpose.

Day 12: I will seek mentors and role models who can guide and support me as I pursue my goals.

Day 13: I will celebrate my progress and accomplishments as I work towards my purpose.

Day 14: I will be resilient in the face of adversity and stay focused on my goals.

Day 15: I will find meaning and purpose in my struggles and use them as opportunities for growth.

Day 16: I will use faith or spirituality as a source of strength and guidance as I pursue my purpose.

Day 17: I will not let my circumstances define me – I have the power to shape my future.

Day 18: I will be grateful for the present moment and trust in the journey towards my purpose.

Day 19: I will be patient and persistent as I search for my purpose – it may take time and exploration to figure out what is suitable for me.

Day 20: I will stay positive and hopeful while pursuing my goals, even facing challenges.

Day 21: I am worthy and capable of living a fulfilling and meaningful life, and I will use my purpose to impact the world positively.

CHAPTER 2

Building Resilience

Resilience is the ability to bounce back from adversity, but it is not something we are born with – it is a skill that can be developed and strengthened over time. This chapter will explore how to build resilience and use it to overcome adversity and achieve your goals.

We define resilience as the ability to bounce back from challenges and setbacks and adapt and thrive in difficult circumstances. It is essential for anyone who wants to turn adversity into something positive. It is a crucial characteristic that allows individuals to navigate challenges and setbacks without being overwhelmed or defeated.

The importance of resilience cannot be overstated, as it enables us to weather the storms of life and emerge more substantial and resilient than before. In addition, it helps us to maintain a positive outlook and not get bogged down by negative emotions or thoughts.

STRATEGIES TO BUILD RESILIENCE

1. Developing a positive mindset: This involves focusing on the positive aspects of life and not dwelling on negative thoughts or circumstances.

2. Practicing self-care: This includes taking care of our physical, emotional, and mental well-being through exercise, relaxation techniques, and seeking support from friends and family.

3. Building social connections: Having a solid support network of friends and family can give us a sense of belonging and help us cope with difficult times.

4. Seeking out new challenges: Taking on new challenges and stepping outside of our comfort zone can help us to build resilience by expanding our capabilities and developing new skills.

5. Learning from past experiences: Reflecting on past experiences and learning from them can help us to become more resilient and better equipped to handle future challenges.

An example of building resilience can be seen in the story of Jane, a young woman who lost her job due to company downsizing. Rather than becoming discouraged and giving up, Jane used the experience as an opportunity to reassess her career goals and take control of her future. She enrolled in a professional development course and used her newly acquired skills to secure a better-paying job with a more fulfilling work environment. Through her determination and perseverance, Jane was able to build resilience and bounce back from her setback.

Consider the story of John, a young man who faced numerous setbacks and challenges in his life. John grew up in poverty and faced numerous hardships, including abuse and neglect. He struggled in school and often felt hopeless and defeated. But despite these challenges, John refused to give up. He worked hard and eventually graduated from high school, and he even managed to earn a scholarship to college.

John's journey to college was a challenging one. He faced numerous obstacles and setbacks along the way, including financial struggles and family crises. But John was determined to succeed. He leaned on his support system, including friends, mentors, and faith, and he refused to let his circumstances define him.

John's story illustrates the power of resilience. It's not always easy to bounce back from adversity, but it is possible. In this chapter, we will explore strategies for building strength, including the importance of having a support system, finding meaning and purpose in your struggles, and cultivating a growth mindset. We will also discuss the role of self-care in building resilience, and we will offer tips for maintaining mental and emotional well-being in the face of adversity.

One real-life example of building resilience can be seen in the story of a student who was determined to get to class despite facing a seemingly insurmountable obstacle. When this student couldn't afford the bus fare to get to class, he didn't give up or let his disappointment hold him back. Instead, he found the determination and perseverance to walk 45 minutes to class, so he passed the exam.

This story illustrates the importance of resilience in overcoming adversity and achieving success. It also highlights the strategies that can be used to build resilience, such as determination, hard work, and perseverance. By cultivating these qualities and adopting a resilient mindset, we can overcome challenges and setbacks and achieve our goals and aspirations.

TRANSFORMATIONAL LIFE LESSONS

1. Resilience is a skill that can be developed and strengthened over time. Don't be afraid to face challenges and setbacks – use them as opportunities to grow and learn. For example, if you have faced rejection in your job search, don't let it discourage you. Instead, use it as an opportunity to learn from your mistakes, update your resume and cover letter, and try again.

2. Having a support system is crucial for building resilience. Surround yourself with people who believe in you and who will support you through the highs and lows. This might include friends, family, mentors, or a support group. For example, if you are facing a difficult time in your personal life, reach out to a trusted friend or family member for support and encouragement.

3. Finding meaning and purpose in your struggles can help you to build resilience and persevere through difficult times. Look for ways to turn your challenges into opportunities for growth and impact. For example, if you have faced health challenges, you might use your experiences to advocate for others or to raise awareness about a particular health issue.

4. Cultivating a growth mindset can help you to embrace challenges and see setbacks as opportunities for learning and development. For example, if you struggle with a particular task or skill, try to approach it with a growth mindset and see it as an opportunity to learn and improve rather than as a personal failure.

5. Self-care is an important part of building resilience. Take care of your mental and emotional well-being and make time for activities that nourish and recharge you. This might include exercise, meditation, journaling, or spending time with loved ones. For example, if you are feeling stressed or overwhelmed, make time for activities that help you to relax and recharge, such as taking a walk or practising yoga.

6. Remember that resilience is not about avoiding challenges or setbacks – it's about facing them head-on and coming out stronger on the other side. Just like John, who faced numerous obstacles and setbacks.

21 DAYS TRANSFORMATIONAL

Affirmations

Day 1. Practice deep breathing or relaxation techniques, such as progressive muscle relaxation or guided meditation.

Day 2. Engage in physical activity or exercise, which can help to reduce stress and improve overall well-being.

Day 3. Set aside time each day for activities that you enjoy and that help you to relax and recharge, such as reading, gardening, or taking a walk.

Day 4. Make time for social connections and relationships, which can provide support and reduce stress.

Day 5. Practice gratitude and focus on the good things in your life, which can help to shift your perspective and reduce stress.

Day 6. Take breaks and set boundaries when needed, and make sure to get enough sleep, eat well, and stay hydrated to help manage stress.

Day 7. Seek professional help if you are struggling with stress or other emotional issues, such as through therapy or counselling.

Day 8. Consider using stress-reducing tools or techniques, such as aromatherapy, journaling, or colour therapy.

Day 9. Practice mindfulness and try to stay present at the moment, letting go of worry about the past or future.

Day 10. Try to identify and address the sources of stress in your life and develop strategies for managing or reducing those sources of stress.

Day 11: I will be kind to myself and remember that it's okay to make mistakes and to ask for help when needed.

Day 12: I will celebrate my progress and accomplishments as I work towards my goals.

Day 13: I will stay positive and hopeful, even in the face of challenges.

Day 14: I will not let fear or doubt hold me back – I will trust in my abilities and my resilience.

Day 15: I will seek out mentors and role models who can guide and support me as I pursue my goals.

Day 16: I will practice gratitude and focus on the good things in my life, even in difficult times.

Day 17: I will be resilient in the face of adversity and stay focused on my goals

Day 18: I will find healthy ways to manage my emotions and express my feelings in a healthy way.

Day 19: I will practice mindfulness and be present at the moment, letting go of worry about the past or future.

Day 20: I will take breaks and make time for relaxation and fun to help reduce stress and maintain balance in my life.

Day 21: I will set boundaries and prioritize my needs to ensure that I am taking care of myself and my well-being.

CHAPTER 3

Using Your Voice and Actions to Make a Difference

We explore the power that each of us holds to change the world. Whether speaking up for what you believe in, advocating for change or taking action to make a positive impact, your voice and actions can create positive change. We will look at strategies for finding your unique voice and purpose and using it to make a difference in your community and beyond.

It is easy to feel powerless and like our actions don't matter, but the truth is that every single one of us could make a difference.

One of the critical strategies for effectively using your voice and actions is to identify the issues that matter most to you and then take action to support them. This could be as simple as signing a petition or donating, or involving more proactive measures such as volunteering or even starting a grassroots organization.

Another essential strategy is to find ways to amplify your voice and reach a wider audience. This could involve using social media to share your message or leveraging your personal connections to spread awareness about a cause.

REAL-LIFE EXAMPLES

Using Your Voice And Actions To Make A Difference

1. The #MeToo movement, which saw survivors of sexual assault and harassment come forward to speak out and demand change.

2. The Black Lives Matter movement has brought attention to the ongoing issues of racial injustice and police brutality in the United States.

3. The Global Citizen movement, which uses the power of music and entertainment to raise awareness and advocate for global issues such as poverty, education, and gender equality.

Example:

Sara was a quiet and introverted teenager who never thought she had much to say. But when she learned about the environmental impacts of single-use plastic, she felt a sense of outrage and a desire to do something about it. She started by speaking up in her science class and sharing what she had learned about the issue. Her teacher and classmates were surprised by her passion and knowledge and asked her to present her findings to the entire school.

Sara was nervous about speaking in front of so many people, but she knew that this was an important issue and that she had a unique perspective to offer. She gathered her courage and made the presentation and was surprised by the response. Not only did her classmates show interest and support, but the school administration also took notice and began to implement changes to reduce the use of single-use plastic on campus.

Sara's small act of speaking up sparked a chain reaction of positive change, and she realized that her voice and actions mattered. She continued to advocate for environmental issues and found that she enjoyed using her voice to make a difference.

Explanation and Elaboration:

The story of Sara illustrates the power of using your voice and actions to make a difference. By speaking up about an issue that mattered to her, Sara was able to create positive change in her community and discover her own sense of purpose and passion.

There are many ways that you can use your voice and actions to make a difference, whether it's advocating for a cause you care about, volunteering your time and resources, or simply standing up for what you believe in. The key is to find your own unique voice and use it to make a positive impact.

STRATEGIES TO FIND YOUR OWN VOICE AND PURPOSE

1. Reflect on your values and beliefs. What matters most to you, and what do you stand for? What are your passions and interests? By understanding your own values and beliefs, you can begin to identify issues and causes that align with your own sense of purpose.

2. Look for opportunities to get involved and make a difference. This might include volunteering, participating in community events, or joining a club or organization that aligns with your values and interests. You can also make a difference by simply speaking up and sharing your thoughts and ideas with others.

3. Practice using your voice and speaking up in safe and supportive environments. This might include joining a public speaking club, participating in a debate team, or simply sharing your ideas with friends and family. The more you practice using your voice, the more confident and comfortable you will become.

4. Take small steps and build up to more extensive actions. You don't have to change the world overnight – start by making a difference in your own community or even just in your own life. As you gain confidence and experience, you can take on more enormous challenges and make a greater impact.

5. Seek mentors or role models who can provide guidance and support as you work to make a difference. Look for people who are doing the kind of work that inspires you and ask if they would be willing to share their experiences and advice.

6. Use social media and other online platforms to share your thoughts and ideas and to connect with others who share your values and passions.

7. Be persistent, and don't be afraid to speak up even when you encounter resistance or challenges. Remember that every small action can make a difference and that it's okay to start small and

build up bigger things.

8. Take care of yourself and prioritize self-care. Making a difference can be rewarding, but it can also be emotionally and physically demanding. Make sure to take breaks, set boundaries, and prioritize your own well-being.

9. Finally, feel free to ask for help when you need it. There are many resources and organizations out there that can provide support and assistance as you work to make a difference in the world.

Supporting Evidence:

There is a growing body of research that suggests that acting and getting involved in causes that matter to us can have a positive impact on our mental and physical well-being. Studies have shown that volunteering and helping others can reduce stress, improve mental health, and increase life satisfaction.

In addition, research has shown that social connection and community involvement can have a positive impact on health and well-being. By getting involved in causes and issues that matter to you, you can not only make a difference in the world, but you can also benefit your own well-being.

As a young girl, I always felt a strong sense of justice and fairness. When I saw someone being treated unfairly or not given the opportunities they deserved, it fuelled a fire inside of me to act. One specific instance that stands out to me was when I noticed that the girls in my high school were not being given the same resources and support as the boys when it came to sports teams and equipment.

I knew I had to do something about it, so I approached my school principal and voiced my concerns. At first, she dismissed my complaints, but I refused to back down. I gathered evidence and data to support my argument, and I organized a group of my peers to stand with me and demand change.

Through persistence and determination, we were eventually able to convince the administration to provide equal resources and support for girls in sports. It was a small victory, but it made a big impact on me and the other girls at my school. It showed me the power of using my voice and actions to bring about change, and it sparked a lifelong passion for activism and social justice within me.

Your voice and actions have the power to make a difference in the world. Whether it's speaking up for what you believe in, advocating for change, or taking action to make a positive impact, you can use your unique voice and purpose to make a difference in your community and beyond. By finding your passion and using it to make a positive impact, you can not only change the world, but you can also enrich your own life and well-being. Your voice has the power to transform your life because out of the abundance of the heart, the mouth speaks. So, if you desire a change in your life, proclaim it, declare it and affirm it.

30-DAYS TRANSFORMATIONAL

Affirmations

Day 1: I have a unique voice and purpose, and I will use it to make a difference in the world.

Day 2: I will seek out opportunities to get involved and make a positive impact in my community.

Day 3: I will practice using my voice and speaking up in safe and supportive environments.

Day 4: I will take small steps and build up to bigger actions, making a difference in my own life and community.

Day 5: I will seek out mentors and role models who can provide guidance and support as I work to make a difference.

Day 6: I will use social media and other online platforms to share my thoughts and ideas and to connect with others who share my values and passions.

Day 7: I will be persistent and not be afraid to speak up even when I encounter resistance or challenges.

Day 8: I will prioritize self-care and make sure to take breaks, set boundaries, and prioritize my own well-being.

Day 9: I will find my own unique voice and use it to make a positive impact in the world.

Day 10: I will look for opportunities to volunteer and get involved in my community.

Day 11: I will share my thoughts and ideas with others and be open to hearing different perspectives.

Day 12: I will take action to make a difference in the world, no matter how small the steps may seem.

Day 13: I will seek out opportunities to learn and grow and to develop my skills and abilities to make a greater impact.

Day 14: I will be open to new ideas and perspectives and be willing to listen and learn from others.

Day 15: I will use my voice and actions to advocate for change and to promote positive social and environmental issues.

Day 16: I will not be afraid to challenge the status quo and to speak up for what I believe in.

Day 17: I will be persistent and persistent in my efforts to make a positive impact and not let setbacks or challenges discourage me.

Day 18: I will be open to new opportunities and experiences that can help me to grow and make a greater impact.

Day 19: I will use my voice and actions to inspire and motivate others to make a difference in the world.

Day 20: I will be grateful for the opportunity to make a difference in the world, and I will embrace every opportunity to do so.

Day 21: I am powerful and capable of making a positive impact in the world, and I will use my voice and actions to make a difference every day.

Day 22: I am unstoppable.

Day 23: I am indomitable.

Day 24: I see opportunities for transformation; I win every day.

Day 25: I am a conglomerate, Controlling transgenerational

wealth.

Day 26: I have a sound mind.

Day 27: I am in charge of my circumstances; I am more than a conqueror.

Day 28: I am bold, confident and outstanding in all my endeavours
Day 29: I am healthy, and my body functions excellently.

Day 30: I make the right connections; I am at the right place at the right time.

CHAPTER 4

Leading with Courage and Vulnerability

Leadership is not about being perfect or having all the answers. It's about being brave enough to admit when you don't know something and being vulnerable enough to ask for help. It's about being willing to take risks, even when it means making mistakes or facing rejection. And it's about being authentic and true to yourself, even when it means standing out from the crowd.

What is Courage?

Courage is the ability to face fear, pain, uncertainty, or intimidation. It is the willingness to take risks and stand up for what you believe in, even in the face of adversity. Courage is an essential quality for leadership, as it allows leaders to take bold actions and make difficult decisions, even when they are not sure of the outcome.

What is Vulnerability?

Vulnerability is the willingness to be open and honest about your feelings, thoughts, and experiences. It is the willingness to expose your weaknesses and allow others to see the real you. Vulnerability is an essential quality for leadership, as it allows leaders to connect with others on a deeper level and create a sense of trust and authenticity.

Importance of Leading with Courage and Vulnerability

Leading with courage and vulnerability is essential for building trust and authenticity in leadership. It allows leaders to be open and honest about their weaknesses, which helps to create a sense of connection and understanding with their team. Leading with courage and vulnerability also allows leaders to take bold actions and make difficult decisions, which can inspire others to do the same.

STRATEGIES FOR LEADING WITH COURAGE AND VULNERABILITY

1. Practice self-awareness: Being self-aware means understanding your strengths, weaknesses, emotions, and values. This allows you to be more authentic and vulnerable in your leadership.

2. Communicate openly and honestly: Use your words and actions to be transparent and open with your team. This will help to build trust and create a sense of connection.

3. Take risks and embrace failure: Courageous leadership involves taking risks and embracing failure as an opportunity to learn and grow.

4. Practice vulnerability: Allow yourself to be vulnerable and open with your team. This will help to create a sense of authenticity and build trust.

5. Lead by example: Show your team what courage and vulnerability look like by being a role model for these qualities.

REAL-LIFE EXAMPLES

of Leadership Through Courage and Vulnerability

One of the most powerful examples of leadership through courage and vulnerability came from a young woman named Carina. Carina had always been a high performer in school and at work, and she was used to being in control and having all the answers. But when she was promoted to a leadership role at her company, she quickly realized that she couldn't do it all on her own. She was overwhelmed and unsure of herself, and she struggled to delegate tasks and trust her team.

One day, Carina realized that she needed to make a change. She knew that she couldn't continue to lead effectively if she didn't learn to be vulnerable and ask for help. So, she gathered her team together and told them the truth. She admitted that she was struggling, and she asked for their support and guidance.

At first, Carina was nervous about being so vulnerable in front of her team. But to her surprise, they responded with kindness and compassion. They offered to help her with her workload, and they reassured her that they believed in her ability to lead.

Carina's act of vulnerability was a turning point for her leadership. By admitting that she needed help and asking for it, she was able to build trust and strengthen her team. And by being courageous and authentic, she was able to inspire and motivate her team to achieve great things together.

Through her experience, Carina learned that leadership is not about being perfect or having all the answers. It's about being brave enough to admit when you don't know something and being vulnerable enough to ask for help. It's about taking risks and making mistakes, and it's about being authentic and true to yourself. By leading with courage and vulnerability, you can inspire and motivate others to greatness.

CARINA'S LIFE LESSONS

1. It's okay to ask for help: Leaders are not expected to know everything or have all the answers. It's okay to admit when you don't know something, and it's important to ask for help when you need it.

2. Vulnerability can be a strength: Being vulnerable and admitting when you're struggling can be a strength, as it shows your team that you trust them and are willing to be open and honest with them.

3. Courage and authenticity are key to effective leadership: Courage is necessary to take risks and make decisions, even when it means the possibility of failure. And authenticity is important for building trust and creating a sense of connection with your team.

4. Committing errors are a natural part of the learning process: Nobody is perfect, and committing errors are a natural part of the learning process. It's important to embrace and acknowledge your weakness and failures as opportunities for growth, rather than dwelling on them or letting them hold you back.

21-DAY TRANSFORMATIONAL

Affirmations To Help Lead With
Courage And Vulnerability

Day 1. I am worthy of love and respect, and I deserve to be treated with kindness and compassion.

Day 2. I can achieve my goals and make my dreams a reality.

Day 3. I am strong and resilient, and I can overcome any challenge that comes my way.

Day 4. I am in control of my thoughts and actions, and I choose to focus on the positive.

Day 5. I am surrounded by love and support, and I am grateful for the people in my life.

Day 6. I am proud of my accomplishments and the progress I have made.

Day 7. I am grateful for the present moment and the opportunity to grow and learn.

Day 8. I am committed to my personal growth and development, and I am willing to put in the work needed to achieve my goals.

Day 9. I am worthy of a fulfilling and meaningful life, and I am determined to create it.

Day 10. I am strong and capable, and I have the power to make a positive difference in the world.

Day 11. I am grateful for the abundance in my life, and I am open to receiving even more blessings.

12. I am worthy of love and happiness, and I am determined to create a life filled with joy and positivity.

13. I am grateful for the present moment, and I am committed to

living in the present and not dwelling on the past.

14. I am worthy of a fulfilling and meaningful career, and I am determined to create it.

15. I am grateful for the support and guidance of others, and I am open to receiving their help and advice.

16. I am worthy of a fulfilling and meaningful relationship, and I am determined to create it.

17. I am grateful for my health and well-being, and I am committed to taking care of myself.

18. I am worthy of financial stability and security, and I am determined to create it.

19. I am grateful for the abundance in my life, and I am committed to sharing it with others.

20. I am worthy of love and respect, and I am determined to create a life filled with positivity and joy.

21. I am grateful for the present moment, and I am committed to living my life to the fullest and making the most of every opportunity that comes my way.

CHAPTER 5

Setting and Achieving Clear Goals

Setting clear goals is essential for personal and professional growth. This can be achieved using the SMART goal-setting method, which stands for Specific, Measurable, Achievable, Relevant, and Time-bound. By following this method, you can create realistic and achievable goals that are tailored to your individual needs and aspirations.

One real-life example of setting and achieving clear goals is the story of the author, who set a goal of qualifying as an optometrist in the UK, becoming a Fellow of the American Academy of Optometry, and becoming a practice owner. Through faith, hard work, and determination, the author was able to achieve all three goals and earn the prestigious Fellowship.

In addition to using the SMART goal-setting method, it is also important to break down your goals into smaller, more manageable tasks and to identify and overcome any obstacles or challenges that may stand in your way. Surrounding yourself with supportive individuals and celebrating your progress and accomplishments along the way can also help to keep you motivated and on track.

Overall, setting and achieving clear goals requires dedication, perseverance, and a willingness to take risks. By following these strategies and staying true to your values and passions, you can overcome adversity and reach your full potential as a leader.

There are several strategies that can be helpful in setting and achieving clear goals. One strategy is to make sure that our goals are specific, measurable, achievable, relevant, and time-bound (SMART). This means that our goals should be specific and well-defined, with a clear idea of what we want to accomplish. They should be measurable so that we can track our progress and see if we are on track to achieve our goals. They should be achievable, meaning that they are realistic and within our reach.

Our goals should also be relevant to our overall objectives and should be tied to our values and priorities. Finally, our goals should have a specific time frame for completion, with a clear deadline for achieving them.

To illustrate the importance of setting and achieving clear goals, let's consider a real-life example. Suppose that we want to start a business selling handmade jewellery. In this case, our goal might be to earn £50,000 in revenue within the first year of operation. This goal is specific, measurable, achievable, relevant, and time-bound, as it is specific and well-defined, and we can track our progress towards achieving it. It is also achievable, as it is realistic and within our reach. It is relevant, as it is tied to our overall objective of starting a successful business. And it has a specific time frame, with a deadline of one year. By setting and working towards this clear goal, we can increase our chances of success and realize our full potential.

SETTING CLEAR AND ACHIEVABLE

Goals

1. Clear goals provide direction and focus, allowing us to prioritize our time and efforts towards achieving what is most important to us.

2. They also help us measure our progress and hold ourselves accountable for our actions.

3. Setting clear goals can also increase our motivation and self-confidence, as we feel a sense of accomplishment when we achieve them.

Real-Life Examples of Setting and Achieving Clear Goals
There are many examples of individuals who have set and achieved clear goals, both personally and professionally. Some examples include:

1. Michelle Obama: As the former First Lady of the United States, Obama set the goal of promoting healthy living and fighting childhood obesity. She achieved this goal through initiatives such as the Let's Move! Campaign.

2. Elon Musk: As the CEO of SpaceX and Tesla, Musk set the ambitious goal of revolutionizing the transportation industry and making space travel accessible to the general public. He has made significant progress towards achieving this goal through the successful launches of rockets and the development of electric vehicles.

3. J.K. Rowling: As the author of the Harry Potter series, Rowling set the goal of becoming a successful writer. She achieved this goal through hard work, persistence, and determination and is now one of the best-selling authors of all time.

STRATEGIES TO ACHIEVE OUR GOALS

1. Make your goals SMART: Specific, Measurable, Achievable, Relevant, and Time-bound. This ensures that your goals are realistic and achievable.

2. Break your goals down into smaller, more manageable tasks. This helps you stay focused and avoid feeling overwhelmed.

3. Identify any obstacles or challenges that may stand in your way and come up with a plan to overcome them.

4. Surround yourself with supportive people who will encourage and motivate you.

5. Celebrate your progress and accomplishments along the way. This helps to keep you motivated and on track.

Examples:

One of my clear goals is to improve my physical fitness and health. I want to lose 20 pounds, increase my strength and endurance, and feel more energized and confident in my body.
To work towards this goal, I will take the following actions:

1. I will create a healthy and balanced meal plan and commit to eating nourishing and wholesome foods.

2. I will incorporate regular exercise into my routine by joining a gym or finding an activity that I enjoy, such as swimming, running, or cycling.

3. I will track my progress and celebrate my achievements by keeping a journal and setting small, achievable goals along the way.

4. I will seek out support and accountability by finding a workout

partner or joining a fitness group.

5. I will stay motivated and focused by setting a clear vision for my future and reminding myself of the benefits of improved physical fitness and health.

By taking these actions, I will work towards my goal of improving my physical fitness and health, and I will be able to achieve it with determination and perseverance.

Call to Action:

Take the first step today towards achieving your own goals. Whether it's improving your physical fitness and health, building a successful career, or creating a fulfilling relationship, you have the power to make your dreams a reality. So don't wait – start today, and work towards your goals with determination and perseverance. You can do it!

Here are five practical examples of clear goals, along with a call to action for how to work towards them and achieve them:

Goal 1: Improve my financial stability and security.

To work towards this goal, I will:

1. Create a budget and stick to it by tracking my expenses and cutting back on unnecessary spending.
2. Save money and invest in my future by setting aside a portion of my income and exploring investment opportunities.

3. Seek out financial education and advice by reading books, attending workshops, or seeking the guidance of a financial advisor.

4. Work on increasing my income by seeking out new job

opportunities or starting a side business.

5. Stay motivated and focused by setting clear financial goals and reminding myself of the benefits of financial stability and security.

Call to Action:

Take control of your financial future today. By creating a budget, saving money, and seeking out financial education and advice, you can work towards your goal of financial stability and security. Don't let your finances hold you back – start today and take the steps needed to achieve your financial goals.

Goal 2: Build a successful career.

To work towards this goal, I will:

1. Set clear career goals and work towards them by developing a plan and acting towards my goals.

2. Seek out education and training by taking courses, attending workshops, or earning a degree.

3. Network and build relationships by attending events, joining professional organizations, and building a strong network of contacts.

4. Seek out opportunities for growth and development by seeking out new challenges and responsibilities in my current job or by exploring new job opportunities.

5. Stay motivated and focused by setting a clear vision for my future and reminding myself of the benefits of a successful career.

Call to Action:

Don't let your career hold you back. By setting clear goals, seeking out education and training, and building relationships, you can work towards a successful career and achieve your dreams. So don't wait – start today, and take the steps needed to build the career you deserve.

Goal 3: Create a fulfilling and meaningful relationship.

To work towards this goal, I will:

1. Set clear relationship goals and work towards them by developing a plan and acting towards my goals.

2. Seek out education and advice by reading books, attending workshops,

3. Seek out education and advice by reading books, attending workshops, or seeking the guidance of a relationship coach or therapist.

4. Develop healthy communication and conflict resolution skills by learning to listen actively, express my needs and feelings, and resolve conflicts in a healthy and respectful way.

4. Practice self-care and prioritize my own well-being by taking care of my own needs and boundaries and setting healthy boundaries in my relationships.

5. Seek out opportunities for personal growth and development by taking on new challenges and learning new skills.

6. Stay motivated and focused by setting a clear vision for my future and reminding myself of the benefits of a fulfilling and meaningful relationship.

Call to Action:

Don't settle for a less-than-fulfilling relationship. By seeking out education and advice, developing healthy communication skills, and practising self-care, you can work towards a fulfilling and meaningful relationship and achieve your goals. So don't wait – start today, and take the steps needed to create the relationship you deserve.

Goal 4: Improve my physical fitness and health.

To work towards this goal, I will:

1. Create a healthy and balanced meal plan and commit to eating nourishing and wholesome foods.

2. Incorporate regular exercise into my routine by joining a gym or finding an activity that I enjoy, such as swimming, running, or cycling.

3. Track my progress and celebrate my achievements by keeping a journal and setting small, achievable goals along the way.

4. Seek support and accountability by finding a workout partner or joining a fitness group.

5. Stay motivated and focused by setting a clear vision for my future and reminding myself of the benefits of improved physical fitness and health.

Call to Action:

Take control of your physical fitness and health today. By creating a healthy meal plan, incorporating regular exercise into your routine, and seeking out support and accountability, you can work towards your goal of improved physical fitness and health. Don't let your health hold you back – start today and take the steps needed to achieve your fitness goals.

Goal 5: Achieve personal growth and development.

To work towards this goal, I will:

1. Set clear personal growth goals and work towards them by developing a plan and acting towards my goals.

2. Seek out education and training by taking courses, attending workshops, or earning a degree.

3. Engage in personal growth activities, such as meditation, journaling, or therapy.

4. Seek out opportunities for learning and growth by taking on new challenges and learning new skills.

5. Stay motivated and focused by setting a clear vision for my future and reminding myself of the benefits of personal growth and development.

Call to Action:

Don't let your personal growth and development stagnate. By setting clear goals, seeking out education and training, and engaging in personal growth activities, you can work towards achieving your personal growth and development goals. So don't wait – start today, and take the steps needed to achieve the personal growth and development you desire.

21-DAYS TRANSFORMATIONAL

Affirmations

1. I am worthy of love and respect, and I deserve to be treated with kindness and compassion.

2. I can achieve my goals and make my dreams a reality.

3. I am empowered, I am tough, and I can conquer any challenge that comes my way.

4. I am in control of my thoughts and actions, and I choose to focus on the positive.

5. I am surrounded by love and support, and I am grateful for the people in my life.

6. I am proud of my accomplishments and the progress I have made.

7. I am grateful for the present moment and the opportunity to grow and learn.

8. I am committed to my personal growth and development, and I am willing to put in the work needed to achieve my goals.

9. I am worthy of a fulfilling and meaningful life, and I am determined to create it.

10. I am strong and capable, and I have the power to make a positive difference in the world.

11. I am grateful for the abundance in my life, and I am open to receiving even more blessings.

12. I am worthy of love and happiness, and I am determined to create a life filled with joy and positivity.

13. I am grateful for the present moment, and I am committed to

living in the present and not dwelling on the past.

14. I am worthy of a fulfilling and meaningful career, and I am determined to create it.

15. I am grateful for the support and guidance of others, and I am open to receiving their help and advice.

16. I am worthy of a fulfilling and meaningful relationship, and I am determined to create it.

17. I am grateful for my health and well-being, and I am committed to taking care of myself.

18. I am worthy of financial stability and security, and I am determined to create it.

19. I am grateful for the abundance in my life, and I am committed to sharing it with others.

20. I am worthy of love and respect, and I am determined to create a life filled with positivity and joy.

21. I am grateful for the present moment, and I am committed to living my life to the fullest and making the most of every opportunity that comes my way.

CHAPTER 6

Overcoming Adversity and Building Resilience

We will also explore the importance of resilience in overcoming adversity and provide strategies for building resilience. By learning how to overcome adversity and build resilience, we can become stronger and more capable of tackling any challenges that come our way.
Definition of adversity: Adversity refers to difficult or challenging circumstances, such as illness, loss, or discrimination. Adversity can come in many forms and can be experienced on a personal, professional, or societal level.

Importance of resilience

Resilience is the ability to bounce back from adversity and continue moving forward. It is an essential quality to possess in order to overcome challenges and achieve success. Resilience helps us to maintain a positive attitude, seek support from others, and set achievable goals. By learning to overcome adversity and build resilience, we can develop the strength and resilience needed to navigate through life's challenges and emerge stronger and more resilient on the other side.

STRATEGIES FOR OVERCOMING ADVERSITY

And Building Resilience

1. Practice mindfulness: Paying attention to the present moment can help you stay grounded and focused, even in the face of challenges. T

Take things one day at a time. Mindfulness practices such as meditation, yoga, or simply taking deep breaths can help you stay present and calm and can improve your ability to cope with adversity.

For example, let's say you are facing a major deadline at work and feeling stressed and overwhelmed. Instead of getting caught up in your worries about the future or regrets about the past, you take a few minutes to focus on your breath and the present moment. This helps you feel more centred and less anxious and enables you to approach your work with a clear and focused mind.

2. Practice self-care and prioritize our own well-being. By taking care of ourselves and our own needs, we can build resilience and the strength needed to navigate through challenges. Engaging in activities that nourish your mind, body, and spirit can help you maintain a positive attitude and cope with adversity.

3. Seek out support: When facing adversity, it is important to have a strong support system to turn to. Surround yourself with people who are supportive and uplifting, those who can provide emotional and practical support during difficult times. Don't be scared to request assistance when you need it. This could be friends, family, or a therapist or coach. Having a supportive network can make a huge difference in your ability to overcome adversity.

For example, let's say you are going through a tough time in your personal life and feeling overwhelmed. Instead of trying to deal with everything on your own, you reach out to a trusted friend or family member for support. They listen to you and offer advice and encouragement, which helps you feel less alone and more able to cope with your challenges.

4. Develop a growth mindset: A growth mindset is a belief that you can grow and improve through effort and learning. This mindset is crucial for overcoming adversity, as it helps you see challenges as opportunities for growth rather than insurmountable obstacles. To develop a growth mindset, try to reframe your challenges as learning opportunities and focus on effort and progress rather than perfection. For example, let's say you are trying to start your own business, but you keep facing setbacks and challenges. With a fixed mindset, you might see these challenges as evidence that you are not cut out for entrepreneurship and give up. However, with a growth mindset, you might see these challenges as opportunities to learn and grow. You might seek out mentors or resources to help you overcome these challenges and continue working towards your goal.

5. Setting achievable goals: By setting small, achievable goals, you can stay motivated and focused on progress rather than getting overwhelmed by the larger challenge at hand. We can build resilience and the determination needed to overcome adversity.

6. Practice gratitude and focus on the positive aspects of our lives. By cultivating an attitude of gratitude, we can build resilience and find strength during adversity.

7. Learn from challenges and setbacks. By looking for the lessons and opportunities in challenges, we can build resilience and the ability to adapt and overcome future challenges.

8. Practice forgiveness and let go of grudges. By letting go of negative emotions and seeking forgiveness, we can build resilience and the ability to move forward and grow.

9. Seek out opportunities for growth and development. By embracing challenges and seeking out new experiences and

learning opportunities, we can build resilience and the skills needed to navigate through adversity.

10. Maintaining a positive attitude: Practicing gratitude and focusing on the positive aspects of life can help you maintain a positive outlook, even in the face of adversity.

11. Take care of yourself: In order to build resilience and overcome adversity, it is crucial to take care of your physical, emotional, and mental well-being. This might include getting enough sleep, exercising, eating well, or seeking help when you need it. By prioritizing self-care, you can build the strength and resilience you need to overcome adversity.

For example, let's say you are going through a difficult period in your life and feeling burnt out and overwhelmed. Instead of pushing yourself to the limit and neglecting your own needs, you try to take care of yourself. You get enough sleep, eat healthy meals, and take breaks to relax and recharge. As a result, you feel more energetic and better able to cope with your challenges.

REAL-LIFE EXAMPLES

By implementing these strategies and using real-life examples to illustrate their effectiveness, you can build the resilience you need to overcome adversity and achieve your goals. Remember, resilience is not about avoiding challenges but about facing them head-on and coming out stronger on the other side. By developing a growth mindset, seeking out support, practising mindfulness, and taking care of yourself, you can build the resilience you need to overcome adversity and become a leader in your own life.

There are many inspiring examples of people who have overcome adversity and built resilience in their lives. Some examples include:

1. Mahatma Gandhi: Gandhi led India to independence through non-violent civil disobedience, showing great courage and resilience in standing up for what he believed in.

2. Martin Luther King Jr.: King was a leader in the civil rights movement and used his voice and actions to bring about change. He demonstrated great resilience in speaking out against injustice and inequality.

3. Steve Jobs: As the co-founder and CEO of Apple, Jobs was known for taking risks and embracing failure. He also showed resilience in sharing his struggles with cancer with his team.

Adversity is a natural part of life, and it is up to us to decide how we respond to it. By developing resilience, we can overcome adversity and become stronger, more capable individuals. By seeking support, maintaining a positive attitude, practising self-care, and setting achievable goals, we can build resilience and achieve success despite any challenges that come our way.

Overcoming adversity and building resilience is an essential part of life, and it is something that we can all learn to do. By focusing on the present moment, practising gratitude, seeking support and connection with others, and embracing opportunities for growth and development, we can build the resilience needed to overcome adversity and succeed in the face of challenges. So, start today, and embrace the power of resilience to overcome adversity and build a stronger, more fulfilling life.

Call to Action:

A call to action could be for readers to take a moment to reflect on their own experiences with adversity and to consider the strategies and techniques discussed in the chapter for overcoming it and building resilience. They could be encouraged to start implementing these strategies in their own lives and to share their progress and experiences with others. Alternatively, the call to action could be for readers to share the chapter or the book with someone they know who may be facing adversity in order to offer support and encouragement.

CHAPTER 7

Personal Branding and Reputation Management

In today's world, personal branding and reputation management are crucial for both personal and professional success. Your brand is how you present yourself to the world, including everything from how you dress and speak to how you behave and interact with others. Your reputation is how others perceive you, which can be affected by your personal brand as well as your actions and behaviours.

Personal branding is the exercise of presenting yourself and your career as a brand. It involves creating a unique self-image and communicating that identity to others. The importance of personal branding in today's world cannot be overstated. In Personal Branding and Reputation Management, we explore the importance of developing and maintaining a solid personal brand and reputation. We often hear the phrase "perception is reality," which is especially true regarding how others perceive us.

With the rise of social media and the increasing focus on individual achievement, establishing a solid personal brand is more important than ever. A strong personal brand can differentiate you from the competition, help you stand out in a crowded job market, and give you a strong foundation for building your career. In addition, by investing in your brand, you can build credibility, attract opportunities, and increase your visibility in your industry.

In personal branding, it's essential to be authentic to yourself. Your brand should reflect your values, skills, and passions.

Our brand is the sum of our skills, values, and experiences, and it is crucial to be intentional about how we present ourselves to the world.
One powerful example of personal branding and reputation management comes from Oprah Winfrey. Oprah built her brand and reputation as a media mogul, philanthropist, and motivator through her popular talk show, "The Oprah Winfrey Show." She

was known for her ability to connect with her audience personally and for using her platform to promote positivity and empowerment. Oprah's brand and reputation have helped her achieve incredible success and influence in her career. She has continued cultivating and maintaining it through various ventures, such as her television network and philanthropic work.

In developing a solid personal brand and reputation, it is crucial to be authentic and consistent in our actions and communication. This means being true to our values and beliefs and communicating them clearly to others. It also involves being mindful of our online presence, as the internet has made it easier for others to access and share information about us.

Another critical aspect of personal branding and reputation management is networking and building relationships. We can expand our reach and opportunities by creating a solid network of supportive and influential individuals. This involves proactively seeking out and building relationships with others and being generous in sharing our knowledge and resources.

Personal branding is the process of managing and shaping your image and reputation in the eyes of others. It involves consistently presenting yourself in a way that aligns with the values, goals, and vision you want to project. By developing a solid personal brand, you can differentiate yourself from others in your industry, attract the right opportunities and customers, and build credibility and trust. As we develop and maintain a solid personal brand and reputation, it is crucial to remember that it is an ongoing process.

We must continually assess and adjust our actions and communication to present ourselves in the best possible light. By following these principles, we can create a personal brand and reputation that reflects our values and helps us to achieve our goals.

One key lesson in personal branding is the importance of authenticity. Being authentic means being genuine rather than trying to be someone you're not. When it comes to personal branding, this means being transparent about your strengths and weaknesses and presenting yourself in a way that is consistent with your values and beliefs.

Another important lesson is the need to be consistent. Consistency is key to building a solid personal brand, as it helps people to understand who you are and what you stand for. This means being consistent in your messaging, appearance, and actions online and offline.

One of the key strategies for building a solid personal brand is to identify your unique strengths and values. What makes you stand out from others? What are you passionate about? By focusing on your unique qualities, you can create an authentic and genuine personal brand. It is also essential to be consistent in how you present yourself. This means being consistent in how you dress, speak, and behave.

Another critical aspect of personal branding is networking. You can expand your reach and increase your visibility by building relationships with others and making connections. You can do this through networking events, social media, or by joining professional organizations. Finally, it's important to remember that personal branding is an ongoing process. It's something you do only sometimes and then forget about. Instead, it requires constant effort and attention to keep your brand fresh, relevant, and aligned with your goals and values.

Finally, it is essential to be aware of your online presence. Your online reputation can affect your personal and professional life, so you must be mindful of what you post online. This includes not only the content that you share but also the way that you interact with others online.

POINTS IN BUILDING PERSONAL BRAND

1. Define your brand: Think about what makes you unique and what you want to be known for. This will help you create a clear and cohesive brand message.

2. Use social media: Social media platforms like LinkedIn, Twitter, and Instagram are great tools for building and promoting your brand. Use them to share your expertise, insights, and experiences.

3. Network: Building relationships and connecting with others in your industry is crucial for building and maintaining your brand. Attend events, join professional organizations, and engage with others online.

4. Be consistent: It's essential to be consistent in your messaging, appearance, and online presence. This will help you build credibility and establish trust with your audience.

5. Share your story: Sharing your experiences can help you connect with your audience and build a solid personal brand.

6. Be proactive: Don't wait for opportunities to come to you. Instead, take the initiative to create opportunities and showcase your skills and expertise.

STRATEGIES FOR BUILDING A STRONG PERSONAL BRAND

1. Identify your target audience: Who do you want to reach with your message? Understanding your target audience will help you tailor your message and branding efforts to reach them effectively.

2. Define your message: What specific message do you want to convey about health promotion? Be clear and concise in your messaging to resonate with your audience.

3. Establish yourself as an expert: Share your knowledge and experience with others through writing articles, giving presentations, or participating in online discussions. This will help establish your credibility as a health promotion expert.

4. Use social media to your advantage: Social media platforms like Twitter, Facebook, and LinkedIn can be powerful tools for building and maintaining your brand. Use them to share your message, engage with others, and promote your work.

5. Network with others in the field: Connect with health promotion professionals and organizations. This can help you build relationships, learn from others, and stay up to date on the latest developments in the field.

6. Consistency is key to building a solid personal brand. Make sure you're messaging and branding efforts are consistent across all platforms and channels.

7. Monitor your online presence: Keep track of what others say about you online. This can help you identify areas where you may need to improve your brand.

21 DAYS AFFIRMATIONS

To Help You Build And Maintain A Solid Personal Brand

Day 1. I am confident in my unique skills and abilities.

Day 2. I am constantly learning and growing.Day

Day 3. I am consistent in my messaging and online presence.

Day 4. I am authentic and genuine in my interactions.

Day 5. I am proactive in creating opportunities for myself.

Day 6. I am open to new experiences and learning from others.

Day 7. I am unapologetically myself.

Day 8. I am not afraid to take risks and try new things.

Day 9. I am a valuable asset to any team or organization.

Day 10. I am always looking for ways to improve myself.

Day 11. I am passionate about what I do, and it shows in my work.

Day 12. I am a strong and confident leader.

Day 13. I am respected and admired by my peers and colleagues.

Day 14. I am a trusted and reliable resource for others.

Day 15. I am a valuable contributor to any project or team.

Day 16. I am skilled at building and maintaining relationships.

Day 17. I can achieve any goal I set my mind to.

Day18.I am resilient and able to overcome any obstacle.

Day 19. I am honoured, and I am a personality of influence in my field of expertise.

Day 20. I am dedicated to building a strong and successful personal brand.

Day 21. I am worthy of respect and admiration for my skills and talents.

Call to action:

1. **Take some time to reflect on your brand and reputation.**
2. **Identify your unique strengths and values and start building a solid personal brand by consistently presenting yourself.**
3. **Decide to expand your network and be mindful of your online presence.**

By taking these steps, you can build and maintain a positive reputation that will help you succeed personally and professionally.

CHAPTER 8

Networking and Building Relationships

Networking is building relationships with others in your industry or field of interest. Networking and building relationships are crucial for personal and professional growth. Networking is vital because it helps you build a network of contacts who can provide valuable resources, advice, and opportunities.

Some strategies for networking include attending events and conferences, joining professional organizations, and engaging with others online through platforms like LinkedIn. It's also important to be authentic and genuine in your interactions and to follow up with connections.

One of the key ways to succeed in any field is to have a strong network of supportive and influential individuals. This can open doors to new opportunities, provide valuable resources and advice, and offer community and support.

But building relationships isn't just about adding people to your contacts list. It's about genuine connection and mutual benefit. To effectively network and build relationships, it's essential to be authentic, attentive, and give value to others.

REAL-LIFE EXAMPLES

Some examples of successful networking include reaching out to a mentor for guidance, attending a networking event and connecting with other professionals, and joining a professional organization and participating in its affairs and activities.

One thought-provoking real-life story that illustrates the importance of networking and building relationships is the story of Sophie, a young lawyer struggling to find her footing in a competitive industry. Despite her hard work and dedication, she needed help getting noticed and landing new clients. Feeling discouraged and alone, Sophie reached out to a mentor for guidance. Her mentor, a successful lawyer with a vast network, encouraged her to build relationships with other professionals in her field.

At first, Sophie hesitated but decided to take the advice and start attending industry events and reaching out to potential connections.
Through networking, Sophie could make valuable connections and land new clients. She also found community and support within her industry, which helped boost her confidence and motivation.

Sophie's story shows the power of networking and building relationships in achieving personal and professional growth. Appreciating the value of connecting with others and being proactive in building and maintaining relationships is essential.

Life lessons embedded in the chapter on building networks and relationships:

1. **The power of relationships**: Building solid relationships is essential for personal and professional success.

2. **The importance of networking**: Networking allows you to connect with others who can help you achieve your goals.

3. **The value of collaboration**: Working with others can help you achieve more than you could on your own.

4. **The role of communication**: Effective communication is key to building and maintaining relationships.

5. **The importance of authenticity**: Being authentic and genuine in your relationships helps build trust and rapport.

6. **The role of vulnerability**: Being vulnerable allows you to build deeper and more meaningful relationships.

Call to Action:

The call to action could be for readers to start building their networks by reaching out to people in their field or industry, joining professional organizations, attending networking events, and building relationships with mentors and other influential individuals. The call to action could also encourage readers to take advantage of online networking platforms and tools, such as LinkedIn and social media, to expand their networks and make connections with like-minded individuals. Additionally, the call to action could encourage readers to focus on building strong, authentic relationships and being valuable members of their networks by offering help, support, and resources to others.

As we come to the end of this book, we hope that it has provided you with the tools and inspiration to embrace adversity as an opportunity for growth and become a leader in your own life.

Remember that adversity is not something to be feared or avoided but rather an opportunity to learn, grow, and become stronger. Stay focused on your purpose and goals, and use your voice and actions to make a positive impact in the world. Cultivate resilience, emotional intelligence, and a sense of vulnerability to help you navigate through difficult times and emerge stronger on the other side.

Most importantly, always continue learning and growing as an individual. Keep seeking out new experiences and challenges, and stay open to the possibilities that life has to offer. We hope that this book has provided a starting point on your journey of transformation and that you will continue to rise from the ashes and reach your full potential. Thank you for reading.

We leave readers with a final call to action, urging them to take the first step towards their own transformation and growth. Whether it's finding your purpose, building resilience, using your voice and actions to make a difference, or setting and achieving clear goals, we encourage readers to take that first step and start their journey towards a fulfilling and meaningful life. We believe that by doing so, they will rise like a phoenix from the ashes and become a leader who leaves a lasting impact and influence on the world.

CONTINUING THE JOURNEY

As we come to the end of our book, we want to take a moment to revisit some of the key themes and takeaways.

Throughout the book, we have explored the transformative power of overcoming adversity and becoming a leader. We have seen how adversity can serve as a catalyst for growth and change and how resilience and a clear sense of purpose can help us navigate difficult times.

We have also emphasized the importance of using our voices and actions to make a difference in the world and the power of leading with courage and vulnerability. We have learned that leadership is not about titles or positions but about the willingness to step up and make a positive impact in the lives of others.

As you conclude this book, we encourage you to continue your journey of growth and transformation. Remember to embrace adversity as an opportunity for growth and to stay focused on your purpose and goals. Use your voice and actions to positively impact the world around you, and continue developing your emotional intelligence and resilience.

Most importantly, never stop learning and growing as an individual. Keep seeking new experiences and challenges, and stay open to the possibilities life offers. We hope that this book has provided the tools and inspiration to help you become a leader in your own life and make a meaningful difference in the world.

REFERENCES

Chapter 1- figure 1, Ikigai and dimensions for balanced life chart my Alexander J. Tanchoco, February 2016

Michelle Obama Launches 'Let's Move!' Campaign to Combat Childhood Obesity" -https://www.cnn.com/2010/HEALTH/02/09/michelle.obama.lets.move/index.html

"Michelle Obama: The First Lady's Campaign to End Childhood Obesity" - https://www.nbcnews.com/news/us-news/michelle-obama-first-lady-s-campaign-end-childhood-obesity-n279816

Michelle Obama https://www.cnn.com/2010/HEALTH/02/09/michelle.obama.lets.move/index.html

"Elon Musk's SpaceX Launches Rocket, Lands All Three Boosters in First" - https://www.cnn.com/2018/03/30/us/spacex-launch-success/index.html

Elon Musk's SpaceX https://www.cnn.com/2018/03/30/us/spacex-launch-success/index.html

"Tesla's Elon Musk wants to revolutionize transportation with new tunnel" - https://www.cnn.com/2018/12/19/us/elon-musk-boring-company-transportation-tunnel-trnd/index.html

"J.K. Rowling's Harry Potter series" - https://www.britannica.com/topic/Harry-Potter-series

Elon Musk's Tesla:
https://www.cnn.com/2018/12/19/us/elon-musk-boring-company-transportation-tunnel-trnd/index.html

"Mahatma Gandhi and the Nonviolent Revolution" - https://www.history.com/topics/i...

LIST OF RESOURCES FOR FURTHER LEARNING

1. The 7 Habits of Highly Effective People" by Stephen Covey
2. "The Power of Now" by Eckhart Tolle
3. "Man's Search for Meaning" by Viktor Frankl
4. "The Four Agreements" by Don Miguel Ruiz
5. "Daring Greatly" by Brené Brown
6. "The 5 Love Languages" by Gary Chapman
7. "The Subtle Art of Not Giving a F*ck" by Mark Manson
8. "Awaken the Giant Within" by Tony Robbins
9. "The Alchemist" by Paulo Coelho
10. "The Purpose Driven Life" by Rick Warren.
11. "Sheryl Sandberg: Why we have too few women leaders" TED Talk (https://www.ted.com/talks/sheryl_sandberg_why_we_have_too_few_women_leaders)
12. "The Power of Vulnerability" TED Talk by Brené Brown (https://www.ted.com/talks/brene_brown_on_vulnerability)
13. "The Paradox of Authenticity" Harvard Business Review article by Bill George (https://hbr.org/2017/11/the-paradox-of-authenticity)
14. "The Importance of Vulnerability in Leadership" Forbes article by Lolly Daskal (https://www.forbes.com/sites/lollydaskal/2016/09/14/the-importance-of-vulnerability-in-leadership/?sh=7b2c2b2f28d1)

ABOUT THE AUTHOR

Dr Chibuzor Uwadi

The author Dr. CHIBUZOR UWADI is a highly qualified and experienced UK- based Optometrist with over three decades of experience, qualified in three continents. She has a wealth of knowledge and expertise in the field of optometry. In addition to her work as an Optometrist, Dr. Chibuzor Uwadi is a leadership coach and a passionate global transformational speaker. She is known as Dr. Chi energy, the illuminator. Dr. Chibuzor Uwadi also has a range of professional certifications, including being a Fellow of the American Academy of Optometry. This prestigious professional organization recognizes the achievements and contributions of optometrists.

She has also completed leadership certificate coursework at Harvard Business School Online and Saïd Business School, Oxford University. With her extensive experience, knowledge, and professional credentials, Dr. Chi is well-equipped to share her insights and expertise with others. In addition, she has a reputation for being a dynamic and inspiring speaker and coach and is dedicated to helping people transform their lives and reach their full potential.

EPILOGUE

In the epilogue of "Rising from the Ashes: Transforming Adversity into Leadership and Purpose," the author reflects on the power and importance of overcoming adversity and becoming a leader.

Sharing personal reflections on their journey and how they have used their experiences to become a more compassionate and empathetic leader.

The author encourages the reader to do the same and to use their own experiences as a catalyst for positive change in the world.

The epilogue serves as a reminder that the journey toward becoming a leader is ongoing and requires continuous learning and growth. It highlights the transformative power of adversity and the importance of embracing it as an opportunity to become stronger and wiser.

The reader is reminded that they are not alone on their journey and that there is a supportive community of like-minded individuals out there who are also seeking to overcome adversity and become the best versions of themselves.

The epilogue ends with a call to action, encouraging the reader to continue their journey of self-discovery and leadership and inspire and empower others to do the same.

The reader is reminded that they have the power within them to overcome adversity, find their purpose, and make a meaningful impact in the world.

SYNOPSIS OF THE BOOK

In Rising from the Ashes: Transforming Adversity into Leadership and Purpose, we explore the journey of overcoming adversity and becoming a leader who makes a positive impact in the world. Through the principles of finding your purpose, building resilience, using your voice and actions to make a difference, and setting and achieving clear goals, I guide you on your own transformation and growth.

I encourage you to take the lessons learned in this book and apply them to your own life, as you embark on your own journey of rising from the ashes and becoming a leader who leaves a lasting impact and influence on the world. Through real-life stories, practical tips, and transformational affirmations, we provide the tools and guidance needed for you to overcome adversity, find your purpose, and become the leaders you were meant to be.

ACKNOWLEDGEMENT

In writing Rising from the Ashes: Transforming Adversity into Leadership and Purpose, I have received support and guidance from several individuals who have inspired me and helped me to bring this book to fruition.

First and foremost, I would like to express my sincere gratitude to God, my creator, on behalf of my lovely parents, the late Archbishop Rogers Uwadi and Lady Catherine Uwadi, who were a constant source of support and inspiration in my life and whose blessed memory served as an inspiration for this writing. In addition, my coach, Mr. Fela Durotoye, has been a valuable asset to my development, and I am appreciative of their advice and support.

I would also like to thank Mrs. Udo Okonjo, My MEGA coach, for their contribution to my authentic leadership, which has helped me to deepen my understanding of being an ACE leader and enrich the content of this book. Their insights and expertise have been instrumental in helping me to craft a book that will be valuable and meaningful for readers.

I am also grateful to Vincent Okolie for their continued contribution, which has been crucial in helping me to birth this book to life. Their attention to detail and commitment to excellence has been instrumental in ensuring that the final product meets the highest standards.

Finally, I want to express my appreciation to my family and friends, who supported and encouraged me throughout the writing process. Your love and support have meant the world to me, and I could not have completed this journey without you.

Thank you all for your invaluable contributions to Rising from the Ashes: Transforming Adversity into Leadership and Purpose. Your support has been a driving force behind this book, and I am deeply grateful for your help and guidance.